the JOURNEY with the MASTER

EVA BELL WERBER

DeVorss Publications

The Journey with the Master
Copyright © 1950 by Eva Bell Werber

ISBN13: 9780875161037
Twenty-First Printing, 2015

DeVorss & Company, Publisher
P.O. Box 1389
Camarillo CA 93011-1389
www.devorss.com

Printed in the United States of America

THE JOURNEY WITH THE MASTER

By the same author:
QUIET TALKS WITH THE MASTER
THE VOICE OF THE MASTER
IN HIS PRESENCE

THIS BOOK is dedicated to those who daily follow the trail into the realm of higher consciousness.

The terms God, Divine or Creative Mind, or Universal Consciousness are all embodied in the word *Spirit* as used throughout this book. Any of these names may be substituted according to the desire of the reader.

CONTENTS

THE JOURNEY WITH THE MASTER

PROLOGUE

THE JOURNEY OF THE SOUL

S PIRIT CAME to my Soul and said, "Let us go on a journey together." There was nothing in all the universe but my Soul and Spirit. The night was crystal clear, the sky was studded with a million stars, and the air carried a fragrance as if all the flowers upon the earth had released their perfume for our pleasure. I laughed aloud from pure joy as Spirit and I went into the night. There was no pavement beneath our feet, we walked on air that was as a gossamer road stretched out before us, and we sang together all the songs of ages long since past.

As we journeyed on, my mind said to me, "Let us stop here at the house of our friends and take them with us on our happy journey," so we stopped at the house, and the friends came out and joined us; but somehow the music did not ring so clearly, and the odor from the flowers seemed more faint.

7

Then it was that the friend said, "Let us stop here and take these other friends with us." We did so and the other friends were singing also, but the music lacked the sweet harmony of that which we, as Soul and Spirit, sang alone together. As we all journeyed on, a fog settled over the night, and the stars were lost behind the silken veil; the perfume of the flowers came from so far away that we soon lost it altogether, and the air became heavy and hard to tread.

The friends we had gathered with us pulled at my garment, saying, "Come, go our way, it is a good way to go." As I turned to go with them, I saw through the fog a dim light. It was the lighted candle of Spirit, the light within the Soul which forever burns, waiting for us to find it. Then did a great awakening come to me, and I swiftly tore off the clinging hands and stood forth, free.

The lighted candle of Spirit then became the light of a glorious sunrise, the fog lifted and a world of beauty lay before me. Again Spirit spoke to my Soul, saying, "When you journey forth with Me, you must journey alone, for it is only as you disentangle yourself from the outward form of earth things that you can make the journey from Sense to Soul. Until you have made this journey, alone with Me, you are not fitted to guide others on the Path."

I awoke and a great peace was upon me. I knew that in the still watches of the night, Spirit had taught my Soul a great lesson.

THE START ON THE JOURNEY

COME, MY BELOVED, let us go upon a journey together. The day is fair and the pathway lies before us, the path which is to lead us to the mountain heights of a higher consciousness. This path will, as followed, lead you from sense consciousness to Soul consciousness.

I would have you, as you follow this path through the pages of this book, learn to recognize Me, your Divine Helper, in all things. Learn to talk with Me as we journey together and I shall be able to point out to you many beauties of which your eyes are now unaware. We shall spend time together in quiet meditation and contemplation, resting beside pools of Living Water.

You have been taught that Divinity dwells upon a throne at the center of your being, also that there is a garden of the heart where you can come and meet Me, your heart's Beloved. These pictures of our relationship are right and of true value. By following this teaching you have learned to find Me close within you and have come to know Me for your very own.

Now I want you to come yet closer to Me than ever before. I want you to know and recognize Me as a traveling companion. Know Me as Spirit within the true self of you, that innermost reality with which you can step forth as pure Soul, going on to heights of consciousness which you have never known before.

This journey is not a short one, for man does not step at once from a pure sense consciousness to that of Soul. The journey will be made up of little daily steps, little overcomings of the faults of daily life, a daily growth of love for the task and devotion to the One who travels the highway with you.

YOUR MAP

THIS MORNING as we start forth on your journey, it is very necessary that for a time you lay aside all body concepts. Think not of food nor yet of raiment, think neither of health nor illness either for yourself or for others. All of these things are not of Soul or Spirit, and it is as such that we travel upon this Path which will lie before your feet. Can you not see that as we put aside these other things, these outer garments, which you—Soul—have taken on with the physical body, they will fall into their rightful relationship to you? They will be able to hinder you not, as you journey on, and when you again need them for your use and daily life, they will be purified, made whole and of benefit to you. I must emphasize the fact that you do have need of these outer things of the sense world, for that is the present plan of your functioning; therefore, keep your body as a fitting instrument for your use. Never forget that I, the Master of Galilee, walked and talked with My Father on the mountain peak of consciousness, yet I also descended again onto the plane of mortal thinking and living.

It is these mountaintop experiences which will enable you to go among those whom you meet, as you go along the daily walks of life, giving forth to them a living substance, helping those who are ready, to start on the same journey which you are taking. Beloved, take each lesson which I give to you as a little part of the journey we are taking together, keeping our eyes ever on our goal, which is the height of consciousness which will be attained as we go forward hand in hand together. With each step forward will come many little attainments of growth. You will have a sense of lightness, pure freedom and joy as with Me you travel on and upward. I do not always promise a smooth pathway, for many times the senses will rebel, and days may often pass in which there seems to have been no progress; in fact you may at times seem to descend again into the Valley of Negative things and pure sense consciousness. But always know that we are together, that no circumstance can separate you from Me, for I am Pure Spirit, dwelling in the Soul, which is you. The mountaintop lies ahead in all its beauty, for your attainment. Shall we not set forth, My child?

Take each simple lesson on the following pages as

a map for you to follow. Some are short, some long, but they will, if obeyed, make clear your consciousness of the Divine Comrade who goes with you each step of the way.

TRAVELING COMPANION

As WE TRAVEL together on the path of consciousness, you will find that circumstances, things and people which pleased and satisfied before, satisfy no longer. At this point you are apt to turn and with a backward look wonder why this is so, and ask if it is right that you leave these friends as you go forward. Yet you seem to find little pleasure in their company, and those things which amused you and made you happy do so no longer. Do not try to force pleasure where it is no longer found, and the old friends whom you have left on another path, no matter how good that path is for them, would find no more satisfaction in your company than you did in theirs.

You are starting on a journey with Me, the way narrows for you, and you will find, in order to go forward on this chosen way, you will have to drop off all excess baggage. Those friends who drag you back, pulling at your skirts, with idle conversation, are not yet ready, nor of sufficient understanding, for the journey you are taking in consciousness.

You need not be lonely, nor full of regret, for there walks by your side One in sandal-shod feet who

has walked the way before you and understands the
human heart, with all its desires and its longing for
understanding. He is Your Companion, He and the
Helpers He has chosen to give you aid and refreshment. You will also meet other travelers; some will be
ahead of you and they will reach back willing hands
to help you when the going proves rough. Others you
shall help as you go on together. Many new joys will
take the place of the old pleasures as you go singing
on your upward way. Sometimes you will hear a mur-
muring echo from the old path which you have left
behind, but as you pause and look backward, you will
see, with wondering eyes, how far you have come on
the path of attainment, and you will go forward with
shining face, clasping the hands of those who travel
with you.

THE GREAT INDWELLER

YOU, MY BELOVED, are beginning to know and
understand that that which is within you, that
which the outer world does not see, is much more real
than the world of outer consciousness. This to which
I refer is the great Indweller who moves and functions
through you, who thinks through your mind and
speaks through your lips. This is YOU—the living
soul of YOU. Within your Soul I, Spirit, do abide,
and as you learn from your soul consciousness to contact Me, even so am I able to think through your

mind and speak My words of love and wisdom through your lips. This thought is worthy of much contemplation, and as we rest from the heat of the day, beside the clear pool, I shall unfold its deep meaning to you. (This resting and contemplating the given word is of most importance.) Never fail as you thus rest to know that My Holy Presence is enfolding you, giving you understanding far beyond the words you have just read.

It is upon the acceptance and full realization of this lesson that your consciousness of power will depend. As you come into the full knowledge that the physical is only the outer wrapping of Soul and Spirit, you will carry with you a glow, a radiance that is like a shining forth in a dark night. Those whom you meet in your daily contacts will sense this inner glow. You will be spoken of as having what man calls "personality" and will carry with you a veritable fount of youth and joy. As Soul you have never been born, nor shall you ever die, and as you function from this point in consciousness, you will have a sure knowing, a deep perception which will color all of the outer functioning of your life. You will find your life on the outer plane moving forward in a harmony such as you have never before known. My Beloved, it is so necessary that we take time to cultivate this inner growth and this inner development. Each day never fail to withdraw from the outer chatter and clamor of the material world about you, that I may renew for you your strength and give you of My Spiritual power.

SOME SHALL YOU HELP

As you journey upward, on your search to gain a consciousness of this higher way of life, which I desire for you, you will meet many who have in various degrees this knowledge. Some know, yet do they not put the teachings into practice. Others strive and long to know more and try to keep the faith and do follow My footsteps to the best of their ability. Here you may stumble and fall into a temptation of which I wish to warn you, My Beloved. As you meet these others, you will be anxious that they stand with you on that particular height of consciousness where your feet have carried you. But this may not be wise. They may be following another trail to the summit, and from their position the view would appear to be a very different one. Where they are in consciousness may be an attainment for them, and you must know that the Master walks with them also. I know what each Soul has need of, to bring it to the summit, and will leave no struggling traveler alone on the path that leads to Home, which is true union with the Father. So do not cause confusion by trying to make them view life from your station, neither shall you condemn them because they walk a different path. I long for you to know and understand these things even as I understand them.

Yet, again, someone may come to you, and you will sense, without quite knowing why, the hunger of their heart. This Soul is by your side on the path, yet their eyes are not as yet fully open to the beauties which lie about them, neither are their ears attuned to the music of My Spheres. Then do I speak to you, whom I love so dearly, and tell you that it is right and fitting for you to hold out your hand and say to them, "Let me help you to see and understand." With this weaker hand in yours you shall go on in love together. Your own consciousness shall expand with every word of help given. You need not strive to seek out the one whom you are to help, for I, the Divine Spirit of your Soul, will make it plain to you. So journey on, Beloved, singing your songs of praise, that all knowledge will be given to you, as well as strength and wisdom to help where I see fit.

THE AWAKENING

M Y BELOVED, as you become still, still with all the meaning of the word stillness, I light a candle behind your eyes. I fill your entire being with a radiance that has a glow unto a glorious sunrise. No man can contact Me, the Living Power behind all things, and carry about with him heaviness, a dullness of face or body. When I am recognized in the fullness of My beauty, all things beautiful will flow into that life which so recognizes Me.

Today, as we speak quietly together, as you come into the consciousness of My Presence, in order that I may direct your footsteps, I want you to think

on this—''There are many Souls but only one Spirit.''
Yes, how true it is, for in every human form dwells
a living Soul. Man does not recognize this. To most
of those who walk the ways of life the outer is all that
matters. The Soul is never lost, but it is buried so deep
in material thought that it cannot function consciously
in the vessel given it for that purpose, and that purpose alone. So the physical body carries on haltingly
and feebly in earth consciousness. It develops pain and
illnesses, it withers with age. It worries and suffers
when all the while deep within, neglected and unknown, abides that which knows no illness, neither
cold nor hunger—that which is ageless, the Soul. This
must quietly await the awakening, for man was at this
point given free choice, either to dwell in the Father's
house or to dwell in outer consciousness.

Man may never permit this Soul to step forward in
its rightful place, in this present incarnation, but will
struggle on, unaware as to who he is, until life at last,
through the struggle, points him to his own true Soul-
self. When he is at last awakened, he will know the
truth that he is a Soul and likewise so are all whom
he meets, and through each there flows the One Spirit.
When he knows this, when he—Soul—contacts the living Spirit and makes at-one-ment, he will be lighted
as with a living flame. Life will take on the beauty and
glory of the Living Presence of God, and man, as
Soul, will go forth as conqueror. At that one high
moment of his recognition of union with the Father,
he has become the true Son of that Father. All his

outward manifestation will carry that glory with it. And so, my Beloved, again let us step forward. Today, no matter how lowly the task, know that you are a Soul, and you and Spirit move and act as *one*, and I promise you a consciousness of My love abiding with you every moment of the day.

INCLINE YOUR EAR

So softly do My words fall upon your ear, that unless you are very still within your entire being, their beauty is lost to you. Yet if you will practice listening for My voice, you will find that it is always there, no matter where you are nor what the circumstances are. Always in the outer world, on the plane where you function in physical form, problems will arise which puzzle and confound you, for which you will feel the need of help. Learn at such a time, Beloved, to quietly still the mind, incline your ear and gently shall I speak to you the word of counsel which you will need at that moment. Likewise when you are caught up in outer conditions of annoying circumstances—wait—and gently will I come forward with the word of help and a word of caution, which will keep you from being involved in the negative.

These and many other times will you need Me. It is well and good that each day a time be spent, as you are doing now, in quietly waiting. A time for drawing near to Me, for My love to enfold you in its warmth and blessing. A time when you shall, in turn, give to Me your love and blessing, and Spirit and Soul shall become One in perfect flowing harmony. You can then take up the activities of the day and meet its problems and solve them by My power working through you. But it is also necessary that at all times you learn to listen and to incline your ear to Me, that when you need Me most I will be available to you.

Some expect and desire My voice to come in a loud, clear tone, but I am not thus. My voice is even as the sighing of the wind in the treetops, the soft drip of summer rain, the sweet, elusive perfume of the rose. It is better so, for the world has enough of loud speaking; I need not add to its clamor. And so My Beloved, you must learn to listen; then I shall never fail you. Always will you feel my tender guidance and protecting love, until you come to know a close fellowship of Soul and Spirit, which you can gain in no other way, and the outer will for you take on the beauty of the Presence.

THE HIGHEST PERCEPTION

THE FINEST WORK is not done with heavy machinery. Even so it is with your development. The highest perception is of extreme fineness and of a high, light quality. You can only acquire this perception, My child, by time spent realizing My Presence. Only by infinite patience can you come to hear My voice.

As I told you in a former lesson, I do not speak loudly, nor do I clamor at the door of your senses. You must still all outer thinking and emotions; then can I speak, and you shall perceive that it is I, your Lord and Master. It is I, Spirit, speaking to the soul of you. I only speak through a stilled mind, even as the lovely tree on the bank can only mirror its beauty in a quiet pool. I would indeed have you cultivate this finer perception. Upon its cultivation you will find that it will become easy at any time and in any place to still the mind. It is then, as you go your way, you shall ever be conscious of guidance and of My Loving Presence. No matter what shall arise in the outer, you will have at close hand My wisdom for your use.

Never feel that it is your own wisdom, or rather the wisdom of your outer mind, because it comes so quickly. At times you shall have such an instant response to your sense of need for guidance that it will appear to be your thought, but behind that thought My voice has spoken. This, Beloved, is true oneness. This is true right action. This is truly walking with your hand in Mine. When this perception is established, you will have come far up the sunlit path with your Lord. The day lies before you full of many little tasks. Put this lesson into practice, listening often to the sweet whisper in your Soul.

EXPRESS YOUR LOVE

M Y CHILD, as you love those others whom you meet on the path, you best express your love for Me. Love is never static. Loud proclamations do not denote love. It is the little smile, the tender thoughtfulness, the cup of water given. These things do I accept as signs of your true love for Me. You can, if you listen, hear Me say, "It is well, I know you love Me, for today I saw you smile in love at another one made in My image. Today I know you recognized Me in those whom you met on the path, and as you held out your hand in helpfulness, it was an expression of your love for Me." It is hard just to sit and feel love for any person or any thing. Yes, true love is a feeling, an emotion, but if there were never action behind it, the feeling would be of no benefit to Me or to anyone. At times it is true that a great surge of love will appear to rise within you. That emotion is kindled by the love you have expressed outwardly. So never fear, as you give out love, I shall recognize it. As love returns again to you, it shall bless the giver, and you will know it to be of the Father and from His storehouse. I pour My love into the heart that empties itself in turn to My other children.

MAKE NO SEPARATION

A S YOU GO about your daily tasks, you are responsible for seeing My image and likeness in those whom you meet. If you see not this image, how can you be conscious that this image lies within you, how can you say, "I and my Father are one"? You cannot say that you carry within your Soul that which enfolds you with love and tenderness if you deny the privilege to another. As there is only One, He must be that same One. Strive to have no feeling of separation with any other being. If you separate them into one class and yourself into another, you at the same time separate yourself in consciousness from the Father.

This sense of true oneness is not an easy point at which to arrive. By quiet meditation with Me, by a giving out of the love which I give so freely to you, by knowing that the Father is indivisible, you shall begin to acquire the true sense of at-one-ment, not only with the Father but with all your fellowmen. You will realize that you are only a small portion of the ocean of life and that those you meet are likewise a part.

This shall become a way of life for you, and then shall there be no stopping of the Father's *overflowing blessings*. All that comes to you will come from His great storehouse of love, and every desire of your heart will be made manifest. You say how wonderful would be the world if all men lived by this rule. Yes, how wonderful indeed. But for that you are not held responsible. Learn the secret within your own heart and it will be for you and those whom you contact the world which you want it to be.

FAITH AND BELIEVING

COME, MY CHILD, for a few moments with Me in the stillness before we start on our journey into the day which lies before us. You are learning that My voice is low and sweet within you and that your faintest whisper of need meets My ear. There is no need to shout and implore on bended knee for what you need or desire. As you practice My Presence, it shall begin to be that even the faintest thought of need desired by you shall be answered before you have ever asked. My holy word given to man so many years ago is *"Ask in faith and believe."* What is faith and what is believing? I tell you now, the highest knowledge that can come to you is the sure knowing of the Presence within. When you have found the union of you, Soul, with Me, Spirit, within you and have come into the full realization that we are *one* and inseparable, that is true belief and sure knowing. When you have reached this point in development, when you have once known the joy of this union, all the arguments of the world cannot take it away. It is like a lovely bird singing within your heart, and no matter if clouds gather, either within or without, nothing can obscure the sunlight of His Presence.

That, My Beloved, is what it means to truly believe. As for faith, when you have this sure knowing, there can be no lack of faith. You know your Master is ever present, ever watchful for all your needs. As you walk in this assurance, you will find it true that *before you call I shall answer.* How worthwhile is the journey, the task of little daily overcomings! I am by your side, and every step of the way is bringing you closer to this time of complete union with Me. Go forth now into the duties of the day, and I shall walk and talk with you on the way.

INNER EXPERIENCE

OFTEN WHEN MY CHILDREN try to make their contact with Me, they make effort; they labor and strive over what is so simple a thing; they think there should be an outer manifestation. In their thinking, some great light should appear, some shining figure should stand before them, or they should have a queer bodily sensation. I declare to you this is not true. As you contact Me, your holy Spirit within, it is an inner experience to be met on the plane of the Soul consciousness. Can you not see that such an outward manifestation would lower the vibration obtained and you would lose the full richness of the deeper inner experience? It is so necessary that the joy of the union of Soul and Spirit, with the consequent knowledge of the oneness, be made on this, the highest of all planes. It cannot take place otherwise.

That which can appear to the senses is not of true Soul value. It reacts mostly on the emotional life. The emotional life must for a time be laid aside, even as must the sense perception. All desires must likewise be forgotten for the moment, as this time of true blending is emotionless and without desire. When you can raise your consciousness to the degree that you feel no sensation from the sense world, likewise no emotion, except that sweet inner emotion of deep abiding oneness with the Presence, at that moment, as at no other, are we truly One. I say, My Beloved, at that moment I can pour into you such power as the world in the outer has no conception of. Then shall you go forth with your senses awakened to all the beauty and joy of My outer manifestation in the physical world, and your emotions will be tuned to their rightful pitch. They shall not be wasted, but you will be able to play upon them as a golden harp is played upon by the understanding fingers of a fine musician. Your desires for those you love, and for yourself, shall be My desires for them and for you, and shall be brought to pass in the healing of body and affairs. And so, Beloved, when we come together in our time of close communion, do not feel that you are amiss because it seems just a time of quiet, peaceful resting, but know that in these few moments you are building for yourself experiences which will manifest in the outer in ways which you do not now dream of; so hesitate not to come often to this, our resting time, that these words may be fulfilled unto you.

TWO LIVES MADE ONE

IN THE FORMER LESSON I have told you how sense perception and emotion, including desire, must be laid aside in order for you to have the highest Soul experience. I sense a question in your heart, a doubt as to whether you are able to completely fulfill these conditions. I have many times before given you rules to follow and suggestions for this attainment, but let us again talk quietly of it, for it is of uttermost importance at this point that you understand yet further the path over which your feet must lead you. Many persons seem to think that by just knowing a simple formula they should be able to step at once into the Presence. They try to do it this way, and often they think they succeed, and do in some slight degree, yet they are missing the highest pinnacle of joy which they might have. Others become discouraged and cease to try and gradually discard the entire thing as just some foolish idea. If, indeed, it were this simple, that just by a repeating of words you could enter the Presence, many more persons would find the way, many who sincerely try and never succeed.

There is something for you to do which you need not do alone, for I am there helping and giving you courage. Each time you carry out directions I give you for daily living among those you meet, each time you forego with My help the hasty word of criticism or the needless bit of idle conversation, each time you give an unselfish thought to someone else, or even a smile where it seems to reap no reward, you tear aside a veil of sense which separates you from the Holy of Holies where I abide. You cannot live steeped in self and carry about with you narrow prejudices and expect at any moment to enter into the Secret Place of the most High. These faults are bundles with which you burden yourself and which cannot be taken up the narrow trail of Spirit with you.

Strive daily to cleanse the outer life of these little foxes and truly do I say to you that you shall find veil by veil will disappear, and as fog lifts from the mountain trail, giving way to pure sunlight, so shall you find that by this overcoming you have cleared that which separates us in consciousness, which is the only place there can be separation. I want you to see that the value of these lessons lies in the fact that they pertain not only to the inner life and its attainments but likewise to your daily life among your fellow men. The two lives must and shall be made one, as they are in reality. This is the full purpose for which you and all others are placed on the earth plane. When this point is reached by any individual soul, all life is raised to a higher degree and the Kingdom of Heaven is nearer at hand.

YOU—SOUL

YOU BEGIN to understand that you, the real you, are Soul, and the physical vessel is but its instrument. It is not an easy task to put the physical in its rightful place, but until this has been accomplished there will always be more or less power seeming to remain with the physical side of your life. Strive today to be more conscious of this Soul than you are of the physical vessel in which Soul functions. You and Spirit are truly one, and when you can function as one, you shall have full control over this physical body. You will feed the body; you will, of necessity, clothe it. You will provide for its comfort and care for all of its needs. You will recognize the wonders of its involuntary functioning and you will learn to speak your word and have it respond to your command. But it is only as you keep your consciousness high above this physical vessel that you will have this full command over it. Never allow the lesser to have control over the greater; always shall you be in the driver's seat.

This lesson, My child, is most necessary, that it be of clear understanding as we climb the path together. Only by a constant knowing of the real you can that "You—Soul" abide in Spirit consciousness, and only as Soul and Spirit function as one can you lift yourself from earth consciousness.

This earth consciousness is that which sees strife all about you. It plunges you into affairs which concern you not at all. It causes you to try often to do for other Souls that which only they can do for themselves. It is world consciousness which causes you to run hither and thither wasting time and energy— but I hear you say to Me, "I am in this world—I see strife all about me—I see those who seem to need my help, and there are many things about which I must needs busy myself.'' Yes, Beloved, this is true, but these things are for you to see and handle from Soul aspect. The physical will then obey, and from Soul consciousness you will know when and how to help, you will know which is of importance and what is needless for you to do. You will find you do not waste effort in useless running about and will make fewer and yet fewer mistakes in judgment. These mistakes will only be made if you for the moment slip back into the old self mind.

At the moment of your soul union with Spirit you will be master over all situations and none shall be master over you, for you will have cut your claims of physical bondage and thrown off the grave clothes of sense consciousness. Is it hard to fulfill this lesson? Yes, by your own strength. When I walk the path with you, helping you as I do; when you are fully conscious of Me, conscious that Soul is never left to struggle on alone, but that Spirit is always there helping, guiding day by day; you will find the road to attainment grows easier and your Soul will sing songs of praise and adoration as it journeys on its heavenward way.

INTERRUPTIONS

MY CHILD, as we pause to talk together, it will often be that interruptions will come and you will for a moment feel as if you are leaving Me, your

Inner Guide, and stepping back into world consciousness. But do not feel thus, nor allow this thought to disturb you. Know that you cannot leave your true self. There will always be affairs on the earth plane which will knock on your door and require your immediate attention. Be prepared to care for these things and if necessary answer their bidding. Do not be impatient, for it is by this very impatience that you will step from the higher consciousness into the lower. It is only as you allow these things to annoy and distress you that you build the bridge over which your feet will carry you away from Soul consciousness. If you will handle whatever interrupts you, from your Soul plane, you will find, as we resume our lesson, that our contact has not been lost but strengthened instead.

Our lessons need sometimes to be short, that they may be established more fully in your heart. So now I say, read again your former lessons; each is of vital importance as we make our journey into the higher altitudes of Spirit. They are necessary equipment. You would not journey into the desert without a supply of water, nor would you climb a mountain without a staff and proper clothing for the colder air at the summit. Neither can you take the journey upon which we have started, the journey from sense to Soul, without the food and drink and the staff of courage which I give to you in these lessons. So study well each lesson and make them a part of the equipment with which you journey by My side, up the mountain of attainment.

WORKING WITH ME

IT IS NOT ALWAYS easy to hear My voice. At the moment when you seem to lose it, discouragement will come. The world and world consciousness will press so closely that it will seem to smother out the deep inner feelings which bring you into close consciousness with Me, your heart's Beloved. At such a moment, I would say to you, go about the earth tasks which seem so pressing. Do not feel you have no inner light, neither fear, for the light is truly there, ever burning. I am still the very You of you. It is only that the outer has for a short time come into prominence in your consciousness.

As you go about the duties of the day, doing them well and faithfully, know that each task well done is done by Me working with you from the high point of My consciousness. This is the point of consciousness which I covet for you. Each thing that you do cheerfully and happily is likewise done with My blessing. It is not for you to spend long hours sitting in silent communion with your Soul self; I would not have it so. As long as you function on the outer plane you must perform the work of that plane and deal with the physical. Your mind must be clear and keen. If by knowing this you do the things which are before you to do, you need never fear, because you are doing them by My inner light, and all that you touch will be glorified by the Presence. So carry on with your present apparent duties, for we work as One, which we so truly are, no matter on which plane you function. My blessing is with you each moment of the day. The real You is never touched. This is a fact which at times is hard to understand, for the world seems so very near and so very real. As often happens, the telephone will ring, there will be an apparent break in your time of quietness alone with Me. For a time it seems necessary that you meet the demands of outer things. If you can realize that the real You is never apart from Me, that in a second's turning you are again in Soul consciousness, you will gain much in poise, patience and understanding. Always remember that the greater number of those with whom you walk the path of the world do not have the understanding which you have, they know naught of meditation, and in order that you are to them a friend and helper you must meet them on their level of understanding. This shall not hinder your progress, this patient understanding. As told to you in a former lesson, and needs must be repeated here in order that it be fully understood, the thing which will hinder you will be impatience and a feeling of annoyance. You may feel that now your meditation is broken and it is of no use to try, for something always happens when you do. That is the thought that will hinder, for by that thought you will be saying that to you there is a point of separation between us.

Likewise is this true in all physical conditions. When troublesome things seem to occur in the physical body, always stand steady in your consciousness, knowing that after all the real You of you is never touched, that nothing can happen to the Soul—YOU—as the physical is but that which is used by the Soul, and whatever seems to hinder will be taken care of from the high point of Soul consciousness, and I, Spirit, working through you—Soul—will adjust the outer condition and circumstance, whatever it happens to be.

There is a most important lesson in this for you. Earth's lessons must be learned. If they were not necessary, you would not have been placed on the earth plane. The Soul is given a body in order that it be taught the right use of it. You are surrounded by earth conditions that you may learn the strength and power of Soul, by handling them with Soul wisdom and knowledge. So, Beloved, be patient, not only with others but also with yourself. Only know that it is necessary to be conscious of the Holy Presence and you will find that you will go calmly on your upward way, making full use of all experiences which come to you. Know that at this moment you are in your rightful place and that the Presence is there also.

THE WHITE MAGNOLIA

AS WE HOLD our quiet meditation this morning, I would have you picture, as if held in your hand, the beautiful bud of a white magnolia blossom. In truth, it has not yet reached the stage of beauty and you see it as just a long greenish brown bud, but as you look upon it, you will see that it begins to grow, just as your consciousness begins to grow from your first moment of recognition with Me. The bud begins to show a creamy white, even as does your Soul change as it begins to recognize itself. Gradually the bud begins to swell and petals appear. Watch it now as it unfolds, waxy petal by waxy petal. How beautiful it now is, a white cup-shaped beauty, and you look upon it with wonderment that such beauty could evolve. Even so, Beloved, do you evolve, not all at once but bit by bit until you are as the half-open cup of beauty in your hand. As Soul consciousness grows, you too grow in beauty of character and personality, and life about you will reflect back to you that beauty which you give to it.

But let us not stop here. Look again at the flower in your hand. Behold, it opens still further. As the petals fall back, you look deep into the heart of it and see there the golden stamen at its center, and as you look, the perfume of the flower is released and you drink deep of its richness, and the beauty of the flower and the glorious perfume will flood your whole being. So with you as you unfold day by day, learning to be still with Me. My Spirit will flood your Soul, and you will truly know what it is to be wrapped about with My Presence. This is but one example of which I could give you many, but for the moment it doth suffice. Pause, drink deep from the rarest perfume, that of Spirit released to Soul, and as you go your way, all life about you will carry the fragrance of My Presence.

I AM YOUR TEACHER

M Y BELOVED, it is I. I who am your very self, so closely does My Spirit entwine itself within the very Soul—You. The day is at hand, another day given to you for work, for meditation, for living freely and living gently. How many different services do the hours hold! As you look back, you see so many phases of life which you have touched. Will the day have given you a deeper consciousness of Me at its close? Often the hours will be sun-filled, flowers will give off their fragrance, birds will sing in your heart. You will meet and talk with others who are like you in consciousness. When night falls, you will feel lifted to heights which you have never reached before. It will be so easy to know yourself as Soul, and My gentle voice will seem very clear to you. But all days will not be so; some days will be heavy with overhanging clouds, a rain may soak the earth, and the wind will whip and lash at the trees. The hours will drag, it will be impossible to concentrate, and it will seem that nowhere is there any light of joyousness; then, My child, is the time to know that outer conditions can never affect you in your inner reality. I am there beside you, within you. The fact of sunshine or shadows affects not that relationship of Soul and Spirit. Learn to feel and know this in the depths of your being.

There will always be, while you are on the earth plane, times when the song in the heart is silent. That is the time to quietly wait, be patient as you go about your tasks, and suddenly as the rainbow appears in the sky after the shower will come the sweetness of the Presence.

There is another matter of which I would speak this morning. Often you may feel that you are held back by some other circumstance or condition from that which you feel lifts you in consciousness. This is as I plan for you. I want you to come to the time when you need no other help, no other personality to give you the sense of My Presence and the great glory of it. As long as you depend on anything or any person in the outer for this consciousness of Me, just so long will there be for you a sense of separation from your true self. You may feel that you must go somewhere to gain a closeness with Me, or again that some one person shall open a door for you to find Me. This must not be. As you go higher up the mountain of attainment, I shall desire for you the knowing that you need no one personality, nor any specific spot to find Me or draw you nearer to My Spirit. I am so the *You* of you, that there is never any separation, and this knowing is what I covet for My children now and at all times. But I hear you ask, and it is well that you do so, "What of other teachers and helpers who are treading the same path, may I not receive their help?" Yes, Beloved, it is right that you should, and their work is to give forth that help. But I mean for you to know so fully your complete oneness with Me, that those others may come and go in your life, and it will not affect you. The road to attainment is a long one and My children on the journey must help, and do help, each other. Those who are a little higher on the trail reach back and help you over a crag, even as you shall help those who follow. But even though these helpers are of Me, never allow them to come to the place where you see them as your teacher instead of Me. I am your teacher, I am your guide, your instant and constant companion. Come, now, the day lies before us, with its many duties. I bless you as we go on our way.

WORK TOWARD THE SUMMIT

THIS THING of building a consciousness, My child, is not done quickly, nor is it always easily accomplished. As a great building is wrought stone by stone and with days of labor by many people, so is consciousness built. Your consciousness is built by the help of many others. Those whom you love help to build it, and the love you give to them is like unto the great love which I give to you. The ones you meet who annoy and distress you bring you opportunity to overcome the little traits which tend to separate you in your thought from Me. They all play a part in the tapestry of your life. The finished building is that toward which the labor is directed. So it is with you. Never lose sight of your goal, which is union with Soul, which is You and Spirit.

Day by day you overcome with My help the little

negative traits of your character. Day by day you fall into negative thought, but strive to overcome it. This is the way that you are building your consciousness, this is the way you are climbing the trail with Me. You must keep your eye on the goal, ever doing the things which will lead to the attainment of your purpose. Every time you repress a sharp word, or give a cup of cold water, recognizing Me in the one to whom you give it, you have added another brick to the building called *Higher Consciousness.*

So do not be discouraged, but work quietly and surely, knowing that you do not walk alone, for I, who hold you so dear a part of Myself, am always there in the Soul of you. Know that my storehouse of love is full, and I pour it out as you open yourself to receive.

THE GOLDEN THREAD

M Y CHILD, I often feel in you a sense of wondering as to whether you have not received from Me all that the height of your consciousness is able to receive. Truly this is not so. As you open your heart and mind to accept these My words, I can pour out more and yet more of My wisdom to you for your use. Your consciousness will grow and unfold day by day as we sit quietly together and as you go forth to put the teachings which you receive at such a time into practice. A child must first learn to walk before it

runs, and so must My children. I give My truths slow-
ly, so that they may be well understood and made a
part of the daily life in the world about you. Many
other lessons do I have for you in the coming days,
lessons rich in meaning pertaining to the Soul life, that
life which I would have you develop. This Soul life
while lived on the earth plane, amid physical conditions, shall adapt itself to these conditions. Yet must
it also grow in pure soul perception and pure soul
qualities. This, My Beloved, can only be done by practicing the Presence. The lessons I give may often seem
to repeat themselves, rather than hold newer thoughts
or teachings. But I say to you now that there is a
golden thread running through them all which is by
this repetition brought into prominence and worked
into the Soul fibre. This is the golden thread of love.
Love is the key which unlocks My golden storehouse
for My children. Love is the door by which they make
swift entrance to the Golden Throne Room at the
center of their Being. Love, put in practice, and
thereby held fluid, is that power which breaks down
every barrier before you. All men have love, though
many times it is misdirected and turned entirely upon
the self of the one who says he loves. This is not the
love of which I speak this morning. The love of which
I tell you is that which pours out from the very heart
center, which floods your being with a warmth and joy
making it impossible to do aught but help where it is
shown that help is advisable and needed. It is the glow
you feel as you bow your head for My blessing. It

is forgetting self and turning ever within for Soul consciousness and development, in order that it may color all your life on the outer plane with its beauty. And so I say to you, Beloved, stint not in giving love forth, for it is that which, if given out freely without thought for personal gain, will return in greater and greater abundance. Love is that Soul quality which you will store up for use when the Soul has no longer the physical body to work with. It is of Me and My Spirit and binds Soul and Spirit together in a never-ending Union. So go forth—love—largely and freely. Come to a consciousness of My Presence often so that I may pour love into your Soul as living water, for that is the true water of life, and desert wastes blossom into beauty wherever it touches, as if touched by a golden wand.

BE POSITIVE

BELOVED, ALLOW ME, the Indweller of your Soul, to take over the living of the day which is before you. Step aside, if you can, in your aspect of human personality and allow Me to function fully through you. If you are able to do all your work from Soul and Spirit consciousness, what a glorious day of achievement it will be. Possibly to all other appearances it will be as any commonplace day, yet within the Temple of your heart the veil will have been torn aside, and you will then have partaken of My glory. The tasks your hands find to do will be glorified, a song will be ever ready on your lips, and you will never feel any sense of loneliness, for truly you will have found Divine companionship; you will know that the most blessed hours are those in which we work together—you, Soul, with Me, Spirit—working as the One which we in truth are.

But, you say, how can this be done, how shall I be able to turn the working of my day over to the Divine One who dwells within? There must be some method for this other than just saying that "I will do it." Indeed, My Beloved, there is a way and there is a key. Keep out all negative thoughts which will in turn bring negative effects into your life. Act on only positive principles. When a negative thing presents itself and you accept it, that acceptance will be allowing the physical to take over. So, the first thing to do when this happens is to close the door quickly and firmly upon any thought or action which is not of Soul and Spirit. I want to show you that all positive thoughts, all things lovely and beautiful, whatever is peaceful, whatever is something which, when well done, brings a glow to your heart, is My Spirit released in you for your use.

This is so important for you to know, for it makes you realize how real is My help and how necessary it is for you to recognize all of the signs of the Presence. It is by this recognition that you are gaining in consciousness. Others without the developed consciousness likewise may do the positive thing and be living in positive ways, which proves how I flow through My universe even where I am not known nor recognized. Man often thinks that it is he himself that is good and generous, not knowing or caring that it is the Great Spirit of all good which is back of his acts. Then he fluctuates from day to day, and it is easy for him to change from good to evil if it suits his purpose best. He feels that the power is his, and his alone, to determine his actions. You, when you know that all you do of good is done by My Spirit, also know that to keep a conscious oneness with that Spirit and its Power, you must drop from your life the negative thought and thing. You, knowing the truth, are held responsible. Love all things which you do and touch today, bless silently all you meet as you journey, knowing it is I blessing them through you. Then, at nightfall, you will look back over the spent hours knowing that you did not walk alone, nor did the physical control you at any time, and as the day breaks it will be a joyous thing for you to be with Me.

THE GIFTS OF THE FATHER

MOST BELOVED, it is only as you develop in consciousness, as you come into the full realization of the meaning of the true higher consciousness, that you ever really understand the words "All that the Father has is yours," and only then can you fully know that you and your Father are One. You understand that there is no point at which you do not have within your being all of the richness of the Father. These riches are not something that is given you for good behavior, they are not prizes which you can win, but they *are* something which you have always had, as you have always had the physical body since you came to earth consciousness. Even so have you always had these riches of the Father, though your eyes have not seen nor has your undeveloped consciousness taken in the truth.

As you possess these things in the inner and grow in consciousness of what that inner possession means, they shall manifest into outer experiences for you. Let us pause for a few moments and take score of what these riches are, in part. These riches which you possess, because they belong to the Father of which you are so integral a part, are all the lovely riches of Spirit: joy, gladness of heart, true happiness which is not dependent on person or place. What could be higher or have more worth? A consciousness of beauty, light, love; the beauty of nature, of color, of form. You delight in the light of the sun, moon, stars; even in the filtered light through forest trees and the joy of love given out and received again. Meekness will you have as you walk humbly and in thankfulness to that same Father for the knowledge which you possess. All and many more of these qualities are the Father's priceless riches, and therefore yours. As you acknowledge them in the inner they will manifest in the outer form, and your life will be an expression of the fulness of the Father's storehouse of love for you.

How rich a thing is this growth in consciousness! How it rounds out the life so developed! My child, with eyes ever on the goal, keep pressing on to higher points of understanding and attainment. As each point is gained there will come a closer fellowship with the One who makes the journey with you.

I bless you now, this day, as you travel on with Me, your Guide.

HOLD CLOSE MY HAND

A s I HAVE TAUGHT YOU, day by day, to find that "still place" within your being where you have the consciousness of being Soul in communion with Me—Spirit—it has become a very real, a very vital thing to you. With the passing of the days it will become more and more important that you pause often during your day and turn within for the refreshment which can be received in no other way. At times the world, and its affairs, will swirl about you in great torrents of outer activity. If you wish not to be caught in this whirlpool, be still if only for an instant, listen to My voice, and even above the din of earth's sounds you will recognize its tone. It may only be as a faint whisper of the wind in pine trees or the movement of a cloud, or the gentle whir and flutter of a humming-bird wing, but never fear that you will not know it is I, speaking from the innermost depths, speaking from that of you which is eternal. Never for a moment close the door to that voice, to that union with Me, for once the door is closed, it is as if you are in outer darkness. In that darkness there can be released elements of which you may not have been aware before. Fear can enter, also hate and distrust; all the black forces of evil will firmly take their stand, and you will be torn and baffled and confused. You will run hither and yon, and there will be no rest for your body or peace in your heart. *But* that will only happen if you loosen My hand and think for a time you can explore the pathway alone. If this seems to have taken place, if it seems to you that there is no light anywhere, come quickly and claim your true union with the Father, and rest once again in His arms of love. It will be hard, perhaps, to regain what you have for a short time seemed to have lost, and it may appear to you that I have even released you to walk in your own power, but this is not true.

This experience will show you how hard is the trail when taken alone. What rocks and pitfalls lie before your feet and how weary and lonely is the way when you are walking, unknowingly, without your Guide. Those of world consciousness whom you meet will have no solution for your problems, for they, like yourself, will be caught in the whirling waters of confusion. So it will be with a grateful heart that you again feel the touch of the Master and partake of His loving fellowship. That fellowship which only He can give you, true Soul fellowship, is the only one which will satisfy; that, and the comradeship of those others who, like yourself, are climbing the path leading to Soul consciousness. Oh! My Beloved! Never forget that we are One and can never be separated. Ever am I waiting within your heart to help, to sustain and guide you. There is never need for you to try to overcome the earth problems without My help.

KEEP YOUR LAMP BURNING

THE WORLD and world affairs press so closely about you this morning. You see much to do of outer activity and you feel an impulse to be doing at once the things which lie before you, but know, Beloved, as you are keeping your tryst with Me, the keeping of it will make it possible to go about these duties which seem so important to the physical senses. Why start on the journey of the day unprepared? I would have you pause and talk with Me, and as you bring to My feet the things which you wish to accomplish, or the little and big problems which will demand a solution today, allow Me to give you of My wisdom.

As you press on up the trail, you will always find others who do not know how to find this closeness with the Inner Spirit, and they will tell you of their problems and struggles and will cry out as one indeed having no hope. Many of these could not, nor would they, make the effort to understand how close is the union of Soul and Spirit; how near at hand is Divine help with its attendant peace if they would open their hearts to receive it. They think of themselves as pure physical body and carry in their heart all the vicissitudes of that same body. It would be a far step, at this point, for them to know that in reality they are Soul and as such have full control over the body of flesh. You, in your heart, will long to tell them, to show them, the way, but in their stage of development you could not help them. Beloved of My Heart, all that you can do is to realize your oneness with the Father and know that, though it is unknown to them, they likewise have this same oneness. By silently knowing these things, by your firmly abiding in the Father's house, you can lift them and they will have a feeling of peace not felt by them before meeting you, a sense that somehow their world has righted itself; and I say to you that any sense of peace or rightness is the Presence of God manifest, though it is not recognized as such.

Go now about your day, ever keeping your lamp of consciousness burning. Never fear that you will not "Sow the seeds" where I have prepared the ground. I shall look always to the harvest, that it will be a bountiful one for My children.

YOUR DUAL MIND

I SHALL TRY this morning to make it more clear to your understanding how I, Spirit, am able to work through you—Soul—and hence through your mind. I feel you often wondering if, after all, the truths which I give you in the silence, and also many times throughout the busy hours of the day, are really from the Holy Spirit within. I hear you say, "How shall I know that these messages are not of my own mind and heart?" My child, what is your mind but an instrument for My use? When you, as Soul, took on the physical body, you acquired the mind also. The whole purpose of Soul coming into physical form as man is in order that, united as Soul and Spirit, the works of God be made manifest on the earth plane. This can only be done through man, the physical being. But in order that man be not merely of physical form, he was given the ability to use the Soul qualities which are ever within him, as they are the qualities of his own true self. He was given the right inherent in the Father to select what he wished to portray on the stage of life.

With this ability to choose came his choice of good, which expressed the Father, or his choice of evil, or of mere negative living on the earth plane. And so this wonderful mind with which he is equipped can be used as a channel for Me, Spirit, to flow through, or used merely to function on earth things.

Once you know the truth that you and your Father are One, that you are not that which others see, only physical form, but you are Soul—and as such you abide in the Father's House—then does this mind of yours come into its true estate, becoming My instrument for My use. It is as My golden harp upon whch My fingers play, giving forth whatever tone of beauty I choose to bring from its strings.

Once again you question that you have thoughts which you know are not of Me, and often your mind seems devoid of anything which bears resemblance to Me. Yes, Beloved, this is true; the mind must needs be dual in character as long as you use the human form. It is a most delicate instrument and subject to earth vibrations and suggestions even while at the same time it is subject to My use. You, and you alone, as Soul, can close out the unwise thought, the negative suggestion. Only by your recognition of that which is the highest and best, as it presents itself, can you learn to discern that it is I speaking through you.

This lesson, Beloved, is not of easy understanding, and only by quiet meditation will its full truth be made known to you. It is of the utmost importance for you to know that all that is good is of Me. I am speaking through every kind word you speak. It is My impulse directing every kind deed or positive action. As you realize this, you will soon find you are losing your sense of separation from Me and we are truly functioning as One. I would have you so completely One with Me, Spirit, throughout the hours of the day, that the thought of separation and its attendant negative results would be impossible for you.

As long as man feels that he must seek Me out, that he must come back to Me, or that only in certain places and certain conditions can he worship Me, just so long am I able to function only partially through his mind. My child, there will always be times when it is not easy to recognize My Presence, and that is the reason it is so necessary that you keep tryst with Me, quietly, if only for a few moments each day, that I may, in the stillness, renew My pledge given so long ago—"Lo I am with thee always." These quiet moments will help you build the consciousness that I am truly a vital living Presence which you can contact at any time or in any place, for I am always working through and for you.

You have received well the lesson this morning, and it is as I wish. Bring to Me all that perplexes you or causes you to doubt or to wonder, in order that together you and I may talk the problem through and My purpose in your life may be made clear to you.

JOY OR SORROW

BELOVED, THE DAY seems dark without, but within your heart the Temple lights are burning. The birds are singing though the sun shines not, and within your heart the Temple bells ring also. How wonderful it is when One finds the way. No matter what the outer condition, there is a place where there is always light and Music and Joy.

As we ascend together the mountain trail, My child, you are learning how to feel more and more My Presence as a sure reality for you. As we talk quietly together this morning, I would have you understand that this higher consciousness, toward which you strive, is a matter of gradual growth. I want you to study carefully, as I have so often admonished before, each lesson which I have given you. Each is an important step and will carry you a bit further on the path. Take each one and study to put into practice its teachings. Know that every overcoming, every victory over the senses, no matter how small, every time you understand a little better just what the map laid out before you means, you will have a more positive sense of My Presence as a Loving Guide. Nearer than the air you breathe am I. Every heart throb is a throb of My heart also, and everything which concerns you, My child, concerns Me as well. So many little things go to make up the varied pattern called *Life*. Little bits of work, of play, small joys, worries and disappointments, sorrows, in which you drink a bitter cup. Never think that I am not there waiting anxiously to help you and share those experiences with you. I share all joys and sorrows, be they great or small; often My children turn to Me in time of disaster or trouble, but in time of joy they turn not. They hug the joy to their heart, forgetting that I am Joy also.

When you attain that sense of Oneness which I crave for you, when you stand forth in consciousness as Soul, knowing full well My gentle abiding Spirit, then do we consciously share all things. Always shall you be able to turn quickly and know My face, hear My voice rejoicing with you or admonishing you gently, and when the way proves rough, you shall feel My arms in tenderness about you, helping you and giving of My strength.

This, Beloved of My heart, is true comradeship and what I long for you to know, you and My children. I am not someone who helps only in time of need but Someone who is always there, as part of you and all that touches your life. Press on, do not be discouraged. When moments come which make it seem hard to sense My Presence, know that even then I am there, and soon the mists which separate your consciousness from Me will lift, and with their lifting will come a deeper sense of our Oneness than you have ever had before.

GIVE WHAT IS DUE

WITHHOLD FROM NO MAN that which is due him. In these words, Beloved, there is contained a great law. If this law is fulfilled in your daily life, in your dealings with others whom you meet on life's journey, you will have it reflected back to you as an abundance of all things desirable. Let us study the law just stated for a few moments before we continue on our way. Often we unknowingly withhold from another many things which belong to him. You say, "I pay all of my debts, I owe not a penny to anyone; I am very careful about all of my obligations." My child, the coin with which you repay is after all but a symbol, a material medium of exchange. These things you do pay, to those to whom you are in debt.

Let us talk of other things often owed and so often

withheld. First there is the encouraging word to the one who is struggling to overcome a fault, or to someone trying to grow into a higher consciousness of right and wrong. It may be that it is not your idea of how to overcome the fault, or the way to grow in consciousness, but it is the way that they are trying. Withhold not from them the word of commendation which will encourage them and which is their due. Also, do not withhold the word of praise where praise is due and worthy. So many little gestures of good will may be given to lift the heart of someone needing it at just that time. If all unwittingly you find you have done something which hurts another, do not hold back the words "I am sorry." You will thus quickly heal a slight wound before it has time to grow into a serious hindrance for you both. Do you not see how many things you owe another and which the Divine law of brotherhood requires you to pay as you journey on?

Often in some larger way something is required of you and you have the feeling that you need not go all the way in payment, but consider well what is the Soul way of payment. Also there is another side of the law. You, as one with all others, must also receive your rightful due. Withhold not from your own self the things which belong to you. Do not depreciate. Withhold not the thought that, as the Father's child, you have a right to the fulness of the Father's gifts. Accept these gifts; they belong to you. As you accept and fulfill this law of giving and receiving, your coffers will never be empty and your heart will ever be warmed, for it will be empty of all things due any other and filled with My love. As you do not hesitate to give full praise, encouragement and love, in turn these things will be given to you. In your work, also, no matter what its nature, the physical properties with which you work have their requirements. Give to each its proper care, its proper due. Deal thoughtfully with your possessions and they will serve you well. You are on the earth plane and must conform to its requirements. You are, as it were, a guest here in this outer world; see that you are a thoughtful one. While functioning in the physical body you owe the body certain things —courtesies, I might call them. Give to the vessel in which you, as Soul, dwell its just due. When time passes and you no longer have need of that body, you will have learned the earth's lessons well and be ready to know and likewise obey the laws which you shall meet in the newer life to which you go.

Come, let us arise and journey on. See, today, how many things you can pay to those whom you shall meet.

BELOVED, IT IS I

BELOVED, IT IS I; be therefore not afraid. At times the outer pressure of things seems to take full control of your consciousness. You think that you are keeping fear down, and you really try to do so, yet the tumult of the world seeps all about you and makes it hard to hear My voice, makes it hard for you to know My Presence. Then to yourself do you seem to become a mere physical being, struggling to get along in a purely physical universe. The things and events of the world take full control over you and there appears to be no rest or peace anywhere. Stop and think. Do any of these physical-world things have within themselves power? What in the outer world has the power of the wind which blows where it will? Can man in his own strength or wisdom stop it? Who can stop the rain from falling from the heavens, whether it falls in wild torrents or in gentle summer showers? Who can cause the sun to shine, or to cease shining? No, My Beloved, I, and I only, have the power to do these things. All power is vested in Me, the Creating Force of the Universe.

I have brought forth from My creative storehouse *man* and the physical properties with which, as a child, he amuses himself, creating affairs and situations which he seems to manipulate in his world. But never fear, back of all this outer picture I stand supreme. I have not abdicated My Throne to man nor given My power over into his keeping. I watch and wait. I draw to Me those who are ready and who hold Me in consciousness. Come, Beloved, take your eye and your thought from the outer picture no matter what it seems to hold of good or evil. There is only One Reality, and that changes not. You are held close in the Heart of the Father. You are the Father's child, and these outer disturbances cannot hurt or destroy you.

The Soul, which has always been you in reality, before even time began, is indestructible. As you grow daily in Soul consciousness and knowledge of your relationship with Me—Spirit—likewise do you grow in wisdom, pertaining to both spiritual and earthly things. As you grow in power to handle your affairs from the Soul point of consciousness, you will not be moved by circumstance, nor condition in the outer realm. So rest your hand in Mine, My child. Let us continue on our journey into the day, whatever the day holds, knowing that as you so walk the trail with Me, you walk in peace and security.

PAST AND PRESENT

ALL OF THE PAST experiences which your Soul has had have led you to this moment when you are able to distinguish My voice from the outer voices which seem to fill your ears. How truly have I led you in the days and years that are past, though so seldom have you recognized it as My leading. I would have you turn your mind on the past for a few moments this morning. You see many mistakes there which you have made. These mistakes I dealt with tenderly, for I knew at that time you were not far enough along in your consciousness of the true meaning of life to know or understand the things which you did. The past also held many joys. These were accepted and their fulness appreciated, but even while you gave thanks daily for them in prayer, yet they were thanks given to someone far away, some being of great splendor who might at any time withdraw his favor. Therefore, it behooved you to make the most of any delight that came your way. Sorrow came into your life as ever it comes on the earth plane. This was also accepted as an act of God, and you were patient and enduring, accepting it as your rightful due in the course of earth's events. But, My Beloved, those things lie behind you. Those are of the earth plane and of earth-plane thinking. You are in a new era, you have come up and out of that valley of shadowy forms and misty thinking. You are standing on a higher point of consciousness, the sun is shining on you and the gentle breezes of My Presence waft about you. You, Soul, greet Me—Spirit—as the new day dawns. We blend together as One, and truly am I the Sweetheart of your Soul. Together we go on and up with the fulfilled consciousness that knows no separation.

Your joys are now My joys; they are the joys of an awakened Soul and are from everlasting to everlasting. The things of the earth which touch your robes with sadness are only touching the outer garment, for the real you stands straight and sure, knowing that all power is vested in My Spirit, and you now know that we are as One.

There is also something else of which I must speak. With your present understanding, the things which you might now do, which would draw your consciousness away from Me, will bring a quick reaction, and for them will you be held to stern account. You are free in the knowledge which you have, yet you are bound, also. All that you do or say will quickly return to bless or curse you. So take heed, beware of the little pitfalls of negative living, thinking and speaking, as well as of larger faults and misdeeds. Keep your consciousness of Me steady, and as you go on your way you shall be a blessing to all those whom you contact. My blessings will flow about you as the sunshine of My Presence is known and recognized. I bless you as we go forth together.

THE BATTLE IS MINE

WHY LIVE in outer tumult when by an instant withdrawing you can be in a place of peace? How very real to you is the outer realm this morning. This same realm holds only confusion and discord. War reports and wild speculation as to future happenings bring fear to the hearts of many. Where in the world of temporal things can you go where there is peace? Those who live in this state of turmoil are torn asunder with the conflict. Minds run rife with worry and wonder for what each day may bring. But you, Beloved, who have known the sweet peace of My Presence and the quietness of the sanctuary of the Soul have an abiding place, apart from this earth disturbance. This does not mean that I would have you withdraw as does the ostrich with his head in the sand, or not to do the things which it may be required of you to do in the line of earth duties. I crave for you this morning a calm abiding in the knowledge of the Presence, a quiet knowing of truth, a sure knowledge that you, Soul, united with Spirit need never be disturbed. Even as you view the scene spread out before you, within your own heart there is peace, a peace which cannot be broken. This very peace within you will so reflect on the outer that wherever you go you will be able to calm the ruffled waters. Others will feel your inner quietness and will pick it up from you. You shall be able in this way to do more to establish peace among those whom you meet than can be done in any other way. As I have before told you, I have not abdicated My Throne. Let this be your assurance. On this premise can you base your calmness and quietness. So, go on, Beloved of My heart. You shall not be left alone to struggle with man's forces. I created man and gave him the power of function in physical form. I allowed him to choose between good and evil, but I still hold all things in the hollow of My hand. While storm clouds seem to hang heavily over the land, through it all shall shine My rainbow of promise, the promise that My sun of righteousness shall rise and shine over all the world, and My dove of peace shall fly over all the people. But it will be a peace of My making. I, who hold all men as brothers, shall accept no other. My kingdom shall rule for ever more, a kingdom based on love, trust and honesty. It must needs be born out of strife and struggle, for mortal thought will not give way easily, but born it shall be. Then must all men recognize the truth that there is but One God and One Power against which man cannot struggle and wage war. The earth shall be My abiding place as men in their hearts will learn to find the true Presence. Day by day many more Souls are turning to Me and seeking Me out as their only true refuge. The tide will turn, and again I say the battle *shall be Mine*.

SILENT POWER

I WOULD TALK with you this morning of that great power which is to man unseen and often unknown. In the outer realm, where man plays among the transient things, there is a great show of power, there is great activity. Much is made of the power of tanks and of guns and of all the material things which man has wrought to have and to use as instruments of power over other men. In My Kingdom, the Kingdom of the Inner Realm, it is not so. The sun rises and sets by My power, but it is a silent operation. It pours forth its heat at midday, silently yet with what great power. The fog drifts in from the ocean, silently on wings of silver; the tide rises and falls, but at the bottom of the ocean where its power is generated, there is a great quietness. The seed lies in the ground and comes forth as a mighty tree, and the whole operation of bringing forth is a silent one. What thing in the realm of the material has the power to turn a seed into a spreading tree with its canopy of shining leaves, or to put the song in the slender throat of the bird singing from the boughs? Oh, My Beloved, try to sense My hidden power as it flows through your veins.

Only as I, Spirit, can more and more possess the Soul, which is you, can this power of which I speak be able to be of benefit to your physical being, causing it to reflect the wonders of My Presence. Keep poised and quiet. Much speaking and much running about does not gain for you Power. Only by becoming still may you know Me, the Indweller of your Soul. Only in this way are you able to obtain the use of My power as it was meant for you to use.

As you walk in the garden, feel My power flowing from the earth, and know that I am there with you. Know My power behind all beauty that you see. My power is beautiful and is in all that which is constructive and good. Man so often uses his self-assumed power for destruction, never knowing that back of all that he sees is that which cannot be used to destroy. Be a user of My power, My child, for I give it so freely to all who will accept. Whenever you do a constructive, positive thing which will help another, you use My power. As you do simple tasks well, even so is this force flowing through you. Come, let us go on, up the trail, as your consciousness is open to that which you know is yours this morning.

HIDDEN PERFUME

Y OU CONTAIN within your innermost being many qualities of which you are unaware. These are like unto beautiful bottles of rare perfume which you have put away in closets and forgotten. These are Soul qualities and have always been for your use and your pleasure, but one by one doors of material thought, material desire and impulse have closed them away, and some with their sweet fragrance which you once used and enjoyed have been long since forgotten. In early childhood many of these perfumes of Soul are in prominence. As a child you did not view life from the standpoint of reason or logic. You looked with simple faith into the eyes of the Father. You enjoyed the clouds, the sunshine, the birds. You ran and played, and your Soul was lifted high by simple things. You saw God's face in the crystal pool, and joy ran riot throughout your day. But as the years pass, the child comes down to earth's level, and the bottle of perfume labeled "Simplicity" is put away on the closet shelf. Life grows in complexity, and what was once childish joy fades away as the more material phases of life on the earth plane come into being. There are other perfumes, forgotten and set aside. Trust, or shall we call it Faith. When there arises a crisis and it is time to use it, to spray its heavenly fragrance over you, you have to stop and think, "Now, just where did I put Faith? I don't seem to have it any more."

I could continue, My child, naming many others,

but you will know just which of these soul qualities you have put aside and closed the door upon. There are also others which you have never used or enjoyed and of which you have never been aware. These bottles of perfume have never been unsealed, and you do not know the rare fragrance which they contain. As you grow in Soul consciousness, you recognize them for what they are, Soul qualities, and you will bring them forth, opening up the crystal vial, and release the wonder of their contents for all your world to share with you. Beloved, Spirit, and Spirit alone, knows what these hidden Soul qualities are and how they shall be developed. Only by Soul and Spirit becoming One will their hiding place be revealed to you, and only then can they be brought into outer manifestation for your use. Each conquest won over self and material things, each higher step taken in consciousness, will bring closer to you the time when the inner richness of Soul quality will come forth in all its splendor. Then will you find day by day the hidden perfumes, and you will share their loveliness with others as you go on and up the path with Me. It is as you share these things that you will find more and more the hidden perfumes of your Soul.

FALL NOT INTO THE DITCH

M Y BELOVED, I would have you take care that you "fall not into the ditch" of negative

thinking. As you look about you today you see every-
where the negative manifest. It is so easy to become
involved in it, and of how little value such involvement
is to you, Soul. As Soul you stand aside and allow the
negative conditions to pass before your eyes as a picture on the screen of life, but you, your real self, are
unmoved by it. You are untouched and unscathed in
your spiritual realm. Now let us analyze this for a few
moments in order that today you may put this lesson
into practice. I do not want you to close your eyes on
existing conditions on the earth plane. So often do I
say to you that you are as a guest on that plane of
physical and mental functioning, and as a guest you
must be courteous and not withdraw yourself from
the problems of those about you. But as you do see
those problems of the world, when in the physical you
must often take a part and share them, yet at the same
time the Soul, *you*, becomes not panicky or disturbed.
If I can make you understand this morning how truly
you are *Soul*, and as such you have the help and guiding Presence of My Spirit, it shall bring you a calm
assurance which will enable you to go about your
world, taking your share in its problems, but doing so
in a poised and positive way which will give assurance
to all with whom you work.

This "ditch" of negative thinking is a treacherous
one. It is by the side of our path at all times as we go
up the mountain. At any moment your foot may slip
and for a time you will flounder there, and only by
a steadfast hold of My hand will your feet follow the

narrow, often steep, path into the higher altitude of consciousness which we have started out to find. Often you will rejoice and think you have attained new heights, and it will be true, but at such a time take care, for the ditch is nearby. If you cast your eye even for a moment in its direction, the foot may slip, and suddenly there you are wallowing in the mire of negative thinking and speaking. This will quickly bring confusion and fear. Suddenly the sky, which was clear and blue over your head, will be full of fog. You will wonder how you have arrived at such a state, and all the more confusion will be your lot.

While you are in this negative state you will have much company. This company will also be in confusion and turmoil, and you will not help them, neither will they be of help to you. In fact, each of you will but pull the other down deeper into the ditch. If, at such a moment, you will still the mind and get back to a true sense of Presence, you will find that I can quickly lead you out of your fallen condition, and again, as Soul, you will walk the way with Me—Spirit —in confidence and peace. As we resume our journey, you will find that we walk much alone. Only as you thus travel alone with Me—Spirit—can you, as Soul, make the journey into the higher consciousness. As you so walk, you will be able to give help to others who are on the trail, and in turn they will be of help to you. Then, also, from the strength gained by being much alone with Me you will be able to help someone else, who is struggling out of his ditch of discouragement onto the path that leads to the Father's House. So I say for today, and all days, keep your eyes forward, hold tightly to My hand and to My promises to you for love and guidance, that you may bypass the "ditch" which ever lies in wait for the wandering feet.

I AM TALKING TO YOU

M Y BELOVED, I am ever by your side talking to you, even as I AM throughout My universe, but My voice is heard by so few of My children. I will speak to you this morning about this matter. As you go higher up the mountain of My consciousness, it is of great importance for you to know the truth. It is of importance to you to recognize My speaking and that you learn to quickly obey. You ask now how you may always realize and know for a surety that it is the Voice of Spirit speaking to the Soul—You. I know that there are many voices abroad in the land which may confuse you. It is as with the radio; unless you are squarely tuned into the station, you will get a mixture of this and that and you are not sure whether you have the station to which you wish to listen. So I give you the first rule for being able to hear My voice and to know It from others: Be sure to keep tuned in to *Station Spirit*. Your instrument *Soul* must be in condition to receive, and then you will have no confusion. To keep thus tuned takes constant practice of the Presence, which is ever with you. By this I do not mean that you are to spend hours in trance-like meditation, neither are you to try to leave your physical body consciously. No! The physical body is an instrument given to you for your present functioning. When you are to step out of it, it will be in My good time and of My choice. What I mean by a constant practicing of the Presence is this: As you go about your daily work, learn to feel the Spirit Presence in all that you do. Know that the strength and intelligence given you to enable you to do that work is Spirit flowing through you. Often pause for a moment and incline your ear, and gently and sweetly you will know of a guiding, a cautioning, or a blessing, according to the circumstance which exists at the moment. Again, you shall learn to see Me and hear My voice throughout all nature. The bird singing outside the window is using his gift of song by My Power. The flowers are blooming and giving off their perfume by that same power. All life is moved and directed by Me. So often my children do not ask to hear Me speak or ask for the finer perception to discern that Spirit is guiding and making sure their way. On the earth plane anyone who does not speak to others is seldom spoken to. Even so it is on the Spiritual Plane. As you talk to Me, as you ask to hear My voice, channels are opened to make it possible for you to do so. Then when the direct answer comes to your spoken word, need you doubt that your Soul is tuned to My Spirit? My Beloved, how foolish to wander to and fro in uncertain thinking and feeble knowing. How weak and help-less you feel under certain conditions. At such times: speak to Me—for I AM the very life of you. My ear is never closed to your plea, and My voice is never silent when the ear is tuned to hear. Again, as be-fore, I admonish you not to expect a loud, audible voice like a trumpet in your ear. I come to you gently. My voice is so low and sweet that no one is ever startled or thrown into confusion by it. Soon shall you learn its every tone, and when you do, there will be such a bond of union with Me—Spirit—and you—Soul—that not for an instant shall you confuse Me with another.

I give this lesson now, for it is most necessary for you, in the coming days, to know fully how to ask for and receive direct guidance. As you open more and more in consciousness, so does your responsibil-ity grow to other of My children and your own Soul. The things you do from pure earth consciousness will quickly return to you and must needs be as quickly cleared away before they bear for you a destructive influence. More and more you are breath-ing the air of the higher altitude, and all excess bag-gage of negative thinking and speaking must be dropped by the wayside and carried no further. The Soul must journey on and up, unimpeded by earthly thinking and acting, to its goal. Then shall your earth pattern take on the glory of the heavenly one, and you will truly be living now, in the Kingdom with Me.

FOOD FOR THE SOUL

My BELOVED, as we sit together quietly this morning before you begin the duties of the day, I sense a hunger in your heart for food for your Soul. While I have told you so often, again I shall repeat it: Within, where Soul and Spirit meet, is the only place where the true bread of life is found. Yet I also realize that while you live in earth conditions, where physical and mental concepts play an important part in the makeup of your days, you often feel a need of inspiration and help from the outer plane on which you are functioning at the present moment. You feel the need of nourishment from those who are of like mind and consciousness as yourself. You are given opportunity to find this help from those other Souls who are striving toward the higher consciousness. But when circumstances forbid your getting this mental stimulation, never fail to know that it is, after all, not the essential thing for you.

The greatest power you ever gain is when you come quietly within and allow Me to feed your Soul, for I, and I only, have the bread which contains no stone. Realize the wonder of it this morning, My child. Under no circumstances, or conditions, nor in any place are we—You, Soul; and I, Spirit—ever separated. At any moment, anywhere, do you have access to that food which only I can give you.

FRIENDSHIP

Y OU SPEAK of friends with whom you have a sense of Oneness and from whom you gain a consciousness of Me. Yes, they are given to you for mutual help and encouragement. However, friends must part, but we part never throughout eternity. Let us talk of friendship for a few moments. Friendship is something whose growth starts deep within your Soul. It is one of life's verities. You will meet someone, and instantly there is between you a deep harmony of Soul and Spirit. It is like an outward manifestation of that rich melody. This, Beloved, is true friendship. It has been since before time and is without ending, for it is part of the eternal quality of Divine Love. When this takes place, you will find that no circumstance will ever evolve to spiritually separate you and such a friend. Years may pass without physical contact, you may dwell miles apart on the earth plane, but when you meet again it will be as if time had never passed. Never confuse friendship with mere acquaintanceship. Many persons whom you have known a lifetime are only acquaintances. Never between you will there be this bond, this golden thread that I—Spirit—name "friendship." It may well be that these latter ones of whom I speak will be helpful to you, and you, in turn, to them. Never fail to bless them as you meet, and also allow yourself to enjoy them when circumstances throw you together. They are in your cycle of experience and have crossed your path for a purpose, and it is as I desire. I never want you to feel that because some other one does not have your point of consciousness you must withdraw and walk apart from him. No. That is not living in Oneness or Love. Give of your love to all those whom you meet on the highway of life. Never fail to know that I AM in that one also, and as you are able to see Me in another's eyes, so shall I be able to radiate from you, and as you look upon anyone or anything, they, or it, shall be more blessed because you have passed their way. Within your Soul is the deep capacity for true friendship, and as you meet all with a smile and a silent "God Bless You," you will find the world will give you back your smile. You will draw, as with a magnet, those whom I spoke of in the beginning of this lesson, as friends. Their presence will fill your life with joy of the One who is all love, and you shall give to each other of the love that is eternal.

Bless you now, and let us go on our way into the day.

SOUL KNOWLEDGE

THERE IS A POINT at which mere intelligence stops and Soul knowledge begins. This statement needs explanation and much thought to be understood and of use to you. It is very often hard to know just when this point of change comes and how you may attain it when you need its benefit. As you function in the outer realms, in the physical world, you are subject to the universal thought all about you. You pick up the vibrations and thought waves of others, as the radio picks up many tunes which are on the air. The great part of the time you think you are using your own thoughts and expressing your own ideas, but this is not true; for your thoughts are a composite of all the universal thoughts about you. Even so are your moments of fear and depression; these are also most often picked out of the ether which is all about you. These ideas cannot always be called intelligent, and often they are vague and without any truth back of them. You have no meter with which to measure their worth. You say: "I think" or "they say" or "I fear or believe." It will surprise you when you stop and ponder how much of your time is spent in just such rambling thinking. But I would have you know the secret of closing out these "webby" thoughts, this thinking on the intellectual plane, and use true Soul knowledge. When you can, for a few moments, still the outer mind and rest quietly, holding in mind your true relationship to Me, and the thought of My love for you, knowing that you are truly Soul and as such I—Spirit—can pour My thoughts into your mind, in that moment the change will take place. As you change the station on the radio from one of noise and confusion to one of sweet flowing melody, so shall you change from outer-world thought to Soul knowledge. The confusion in your mind will fade away and I can, at that moment, pour into your Soul My wisdom. I can clarify your thought and bring peace and quiet out of chaos.

You may question if the world thought may not be more practical, as, after all, you live on the earth plane and practical problems must be dealt with. Not for you, Beloved. You are climbing the heights with Me, and your Soul is being led by the Creator of the Universe, by the One who planned the Cosmos, the One who hung the planets in their space and timed each turn of earth and sun. Could man do anything by his planning, his practical knowledge, greater than this? So be at rest. When the outer mind seems to take control, stop and still its troubled waters, turn to the Great Indweller who will allow you to think His thoughts after Him. You know that by yourself you can do nothing. I, the One who created you in My image, have full knowledge of the way I would have you go, and you need have no fear that I shall not be able to make you understand that way. Know by this abiding in the Presence and partaking of My wisdom that you may at any time cross the bridge from the outer thought and feeling to the higher thought of Soul consciousness, which will, if truly followed, lead you out of any difficulty and will enable you to make the right choice in any given circumstance.

TRUTH AND DUALITY

So MUCH in life is dual. We see life, death, good, bad, light, dark. All things temporal and of the earth plane are made up of part and counterpart. The very nature of the mortal side is made up of this duality. Man is both good and bad, sick and well, young and old, happy and unhappy. This is the duality which you see as you look about the world of man's making. He can, even while giving an expression to good, turn quickly and give the same power to the negative thing or act. Often, My children, those who are trying to follow the path over which My feet would lead them wander into by-paths, they fall into ditches of discouragement and seemingly function only on the outer plane where the duality exists. Only the plane of Spirit is Truth, that which is whole and unbroken, the Truth that knows man only as Soul, that Truth which knows no duality.

When you begin to so recognize yourself as Soul and understand your relation to Me—Spirit—then do you begin to live a life of wholeness in which duality plays no part. You function from the one source of wholeness, and draw your help and inspiration from the source of Truth. You look out upon the world and see only the One. No matter what condition or difficulty lies before you, you view these things through My eyes, seeing only Me. You know that these disturbances, while very real on the plane of the physical, disturb not Me—Spirit—at all. As you know this closeness of Spirit, You—Soul—will not be disturbed. I have said before and again repeat that there will be much service for you on the plane of temporal things, where the physical body plays its part. You shall not ignore the problems which are so very real to those among whom you walk, but you will keep poised, your ear will be ever alert to My slightest whisper, as you know that in My Kingdom of truth there is only One Presence and One Power. While in the world, yet you yourself shall not be touched by its appearance of duality.

You will learn the lessons for which you were placed in the physical, and you will reap the reward for these lessons well learned. The more you can sense the Presence and take your help from the One Teacher within you, the better will be that learning and the more will you be able to help those others of My dear ones who have not this knowledge of Me and the One Truth of their beings.

So many are still living in conditions of complete duality. They are battered and confused by the diversity of things seeming to lie all about them. They often wonder what is the answer to it all and cry out for light in their darkness, yet do they seek not the light. Those of you who know the true light are like lighted candles and carry the light wherever they are to those who are in darkness and despair. Beloved, do not think that because you know the Truth your obligation ends there. The knowledge which you have is but the beginning of service for you. You are to go on and up in consciousness and will be held responsible for putting into practice the lesson which I am teaching you.

Through you, in time, many others will come to

Me, that they may have a consciousness of My guidance. So, as you look out upon the scene of duality and cross-purposes, never fail to look also deep within where there is only One in Power, Peace and Truth and Love. From that Source do you draw your power.

I bless you; that as you go about the day you may, in turn, bless all whom you meet. Send Love forth to all the wayfarers on the highway, and I promise you a deeper knowledge of me.

MY HEART OF LOVE

M Y CHILD, this morning shall we pause for our lesson? The birds are singing outside the window, flowers are blooming in the garden and trees give forth their coolness. Let peace be in your heart as it opens to My words and as you feel the Divine Presence enfolding you. Here, Beloved, is the only place where true peace can be found. This My Peace is from before time began and is without end. In the outer realm this morning there is no peace. Strife and turmoil seems to be the lot of man, as indeed it is his lot, as long as that which is purely physical has control over him. In My Kingdom, the Kingdom of the Heart, there is only one law. It is the law by which all things are created, the law of Love. In all the universe there is no higher law, and neither is there one on which man can base so sure a foundation. Let us meditate on this for a few moments. In every realm this law of love is supreme. If man loves his fellow man, there can be no hate. No heart can hold love and have room for any other emotion. Love sits as a Ruler on the Throne of that Heart which is given over to Me. This love has many phases. It is like a jewel with many clear facets; each in turn picks up the sunlight and reflects back many brilliant hues from its cut surfaces. Even so does the heart that has love as its ruler give forth service to all those on the highway of life whom it meets. This love is a power which cannot be confined or given in one channel only. One who truly bears this heavenly love, to which nothing else is akin, pours it forth as a fountain pours forth the crystal waters. There is an abundance for giving, for the more it pours forth, the more it is refilled from the great fountainhead of the Father's supply.

The world was created by Love. In the beginning, God, the Great Principle, loved all things and pronounced them good. Only earth man feels that he can function in another way. The bird now singing his song of vibrant beauty knows this love, else why should he sing? The bright-hued flowers drink love from the bosom of the earth, else why their blooming? If you will take from all nature about you this lesson of the first and greatest Divine law—Love— putting it into practice as you go about your tasks, life will reflect it back to you as a great mirror gives back the image of beauty held before it. Man says he loves this or that, and that some other thing he hates. That is not real love, My Beloved. That love is only a play upon the outer emotions. True love, as I have told you before, so completely takes over the heart which gives it entrance that there is no place for other emotion. You question this—and I make haste to answer. You say, "What of war, disease, what of all the ills that plague mankind? And sin, should we not hate sin?" Again I say to you that a heart that is filled with the love that is of Me has no room in it for hate of things no matter how evil their appearance. These negative things have all been brought into My world because Man does not recognize My law. In themselves they are but the outward creation of Man's thinking and misjudging what is right and what is wrong. If you waste your emotions in hate of these things, it profiteth you nothing. True it is that your heart bleeds as you view the destruction of the negative, and the more it is filled with My love, the more is its sorrow at the blindness of the world. I say now to you that hate accomplishes nothing. If you can look back of it all, back to those whom you know to be the cause of it all, to the first condition which brought it about, and hold for that person or that condition a love and pity for their blindness, you will be doing your part to bring closer the time when love shall be not only the law of the inner realm but of the outer life as well.

The lesson this morning is one of the most difficult ones to put into practice but one of most vital importance. Only as it is fulfilled can I bring about the great eternal plan of brotherhood. It is only by the use of the key, of the Law of Life, that you and other of My children can unlock the great storehouse of good which I have prepared for those who love and use this law of life.

MY HEART AND YOUR HEART

BELOVED, YOU COME to our tryst this morning feeling a tenderness in your heart such as you have never known before. As we have climbed the mountain together, I have been able to point out to you many things of beauty. You have felt My Love and Oneness, and your earth senses have grown more keen as your inner consciousness of this same Oneness has grown. In our quiet lessons we have become very close and very dear to each other. Your Soul has awakened as out of a slumber, and has recognized Me—Spirit—as its very self. You are learning day by day that Soul and Spirit are in reality One, and as this One you are beginning to function.

When you look about you at the outer picture, your heart seems to bleed for the mistakes, the follies and suffering of those on the earth plane. I hear you say, "I never felt this way before." No! My child, before, you viewed the scene from the lower level of the earth-plane consciousness. Soul and Spirit union was not understood by you, and the innermost place of your heart was as yet a closed room. But now, My Beloved, it is not so; now the veil to the Holy Temple within you has been torn asunder, and the glories of it have flooded your being. You have entrance now into the Reality of Realities and know at last the full wonders of your union, you—as Soul—with Spirit—Me. Can you understand that this having taken place, your heart has now been taken possession of by Me? It is no longer divided—it has been given over to My great heart of Love, and this is the love which now fills your being.

My heart is filled with tenderness for the least of My creatures, and as My heart throbs and beats within you, even so do you look upon all things with a love that you have never before known. My eyes weep as I look upon My creation and see that I am not known or recognized, and because of this blindness man must suffer and strive until I am made Ruler over all hearts. Even so do you, My child, look with tenderness and pity on those other little ones. Their sorrows and their pains are yours also, because you are conscious of your unbroken bond with Me and, in turn, your Oneness with them.

We are climbing day by day into the higher altitude of Spirit, and often the air is high and light. It seems hard for you, and you even look back at times and wonder if, after all, it was not more comfortable on the lower levels. There you did not feel so keenly these things which distress and bother you now. When such moments come, I would have you pause and think. Look about you and breathe deeply. Feel the assurance which you now have of My guidance and My protecting love. Feel the power which I daily pour into you and then I ask, "Would you care to go back?" As you have the sense of pain over the pains of the world, there comes also a sense of healing, a deep knowing that, though to the outer appearance the situation is dark, in reality in that temple within, there is only peace and light.

When you start to climb the mountain to a higher consciousness, you can never retreat. Veils of mist have been torn from your eyes and can never be made to deceive you again. You, who have once felt the beating of My heart within your bosom, will never again be satisfied to carry a heart of stone. Each step which we take, we take as One, and as One do we share the joys, and as One do we overcome the conflicts. As One do we weep over those who see and know not what they do. As the Master bore His cross, even so do you bear the cross as you climb to the heights with Me.

My child, I rejoice with you, that you are seeing so plainly the real meaning of walking the trail, and of its costs and its benefits. Your emotions will be continually quickened as you go forward, but always know that now they are My emotions which you feel. Those old, weak human emotions which were now hot, and again cold, trouble you no longer. A warm, steady all-encompassing love has taken their place. I can now work through you, using you as a true instrument in My service. I guide you here or there, and you need never fear that your path is not of My choosing. Again, however, do I warn you. Keep steadfast our tryst, keep your hand in Mine, never failing to hear My voice, for one step aside or backward must be taken quickly forward again, and it will have to be paid for you as you retrace your way. The road called "Today" lies before us; let us be on our way together.

CHANGES WILL COME TO YOU

THIS MORNING I want to again give you a lesson explaining the loss of power which you will suffer when even for a moment you allow negative thinking and talking to take control over you. Before this time it seemed to matter little. You studied, read, raised your consciousness, then went about your work in and out of world thought. You mingled with others in discussions of things both good and not so good; then again you would be still and seem to touch My Garment of peace and purity. So easily did you move from one phase of thought to the other that there seemed to be no disastrous effects from the time spent in the lower vibration. Though you were not conscious of it, these negative moments had to be paid for. They were paid with a lack of complete harmony in body and affairs. Conditions appeared on the plane of the manifest which were payment for past mistakes, though you did not recognize them as such. But now, My Beloved, you are beginning to notice a change.

As day by day you make the ascent with Me into the higher altitudes of consciousness, you are finding that each time you make a backward step it requires payment at once. The mind which carries the high air of My consciousness smothers quickly when it returns to lower levels of thought again. When now you allow a negative thought to fasten upon you, and you give it expression in word or deed, instantly other negative reactions will set in; in the twinkling of an eye you will be upset, disturbed and full of confusion. Whatever you do or say while in this condition will likewise react upon you, and you will wonder in amazement what has happened to make the change. This, My child, is one of the signs of the growing high consciousness toward which you are striving. This is to prove to you that now you are no longer free, in the old sense, permitted to wander about mingling with the negative earth conditions in which you happen to find yourself at the moment. Criticism, also, will bring its results and require due payment.

At first when you know this, you will have the feeling that you will not be safe any more to move freely with those of lower consciousness, that friends whom you meet, who wish to discuss the negative things of life and indulge in idle words, must be barred from your company. This is not true. This action would only produce a spongy, weak consciousness on your part. I would have you strong, with My strength, able to mingle with others who are on the lower levels, able to be about your Father's business in a world both good and bad, yet through all circumstances able to retain your high altitude. Keep true the faith within yourself, keep your eye single, knowing that while those things flow all about you, your Soul stands on a high pinnacle with Me. Then, no matter where you go, you will be able to control the situation in which you find yourself. I am stronger than any situation on the earth plane. As you keep tuned to Me, your Soul will turn the tide of the negative, and those with whom you walk will wonder why it is that when you are in their midst they seem to think and desire to talk differently. As I, the Christ in human form, walked among men, I felt virtue leave Me as the multitude pressed close. Even so shall you often feel the power flowing from you. This will not mean a lessening of power for you, for you will emerge from these earth contacts strengthened and rebuilt in power. Where My power is dispensed to others, it is quickly renewed to that one who gives it out.

As you feel immediate results when you turn aside from the trail on which we journey, just as quickly will you again receive My help when you see what has happened and reach out again for My hand. Do not be discouraged, My Beloved, for you are struggling for foot-hold, and it is not easy. As I told you at the beginning, there will be times when you seem to fall back into the old ways, but the important thing is to learn the lesson which I desire you to learn.

TREATMENT

BELOVED, THIS MORNING our lesson shall be on *treatment*. This is a word so often misunderstood. It takes so many forms and has so many varied meanings for many people. Some who treat wish only self-profit from it and use only the outer form. I, in My Holy Power, am left out, and the treatment is given only by human strength. This is not real treatment, and the one who receives it finds he must return again and again, for there is no lasting effect, as it has been given on a purely mental level. But this is not the aspect of treating with which we wish to deal today.

As you realize that you are Soul, and that within Soul dwells the Holy Spirit, you begin to know that all the power of that Spirit is there awaiting your use of it. This Power, which is Mine, is given freely to all who will partake of it and claim it for their own. When this My Power is used and acknowledged, there will be very little thought of the term *treatment*.

As you lift your eyes to My face, as you know fully the sweetness of My Presence, which is always with you, guiding, helping, protecting you, the thought of treating, in the old sense, for someone, yourself, or for something, will seem remote and of little value. It would seem to be thinking of you and Me as separate, implying that you are in one place and I in another, and by your effort I must be contacted. Let this be not so for you. Know the sweet comfort of My arms ever about you. Know that My heart knows before you ask what is your need and the needs and requirements of those who come to you for help. Then, as you wait with Me for our ever-abiding love, speak to Me the name of that one for whom you would ask help, bringing them likewise into the circle of My arms, and know for them the treatment is complete.

As for your own treatment, My child, when the Father has all, need you beg or beseech that Father for a crumb of healing? No, Beloved! The Father's allness is your allness also, and no mere outer form of treatment can ever take the place of a sure knowing of the truth of our Oneness, of this completeness which is yours.

You question now, "Is there not another way of treatment which, while not this way, is yet true and effective?" I answer that much good is done when by someone's thought for another and their spoken word of confidence in Me, a healing takes place. But whoever treats another must know that they are only the instrument and that the true healing is done by Me. This must be recognized by both healer and healed.

There are many different stages of consciousness, many different levels where My loved ones pause and from which point they do their work. But as you go higher and higher in consciousness of our Oneness, the only treatment which you will ever give is that one of which I have spoken today.

Strive for this attainment of Our completeness, and as you go about your world, your very presence will bring a treatment to all whom you meet. As Jesus walked the dusty roads of life, bringing healing and peace, so even shall you, "My heart's Beloved."

I bless you as you pause for our lesson in the freshness of the morning. While the day moves on and you journey with Me, may these truths be fulfilled for you.

MY ROBE

BELOVED, HOW HARD it is to hear My voice when the attention is divided. The world, and world noises and tumults, so easily drown out the voice of Spirit, and if heard at all it is so intermingled with the upset conditions of the outer realm that its significance is lost entirely.

This morning as we continue into the higher consciousness, I would have you put on My Robe. The vibrations of the heights are rare, and you must keep your mind clear in order to assimilate them, and that the things which you will learn and which will greet you from this altitude may be available for your use at all times. Else why the journey at all, if it is not to make the daily life in the earth plane more akin to the Heavenly One?

As you place My Robe about your shoulders, it seems to you a very plain and simple one, and you ask, "What protection can such a simple garment be?" True, it is a simple Garment, as are the greatest of all things, but as you wear it, you begin to feel its qualities and to take them unto yourself.

One of these qualities is indeed and foremost among others *simplicity*. You will find you put in order your thoughts as you wear this Robe. You begin to discard old, complex ideas of life and its meaning. As you unite in consciousness with Me, you have the fulness of life, its abundance and benefits. As you meditate on this, you begin to feel the warmth of My Robe stealing over you, and you draw its folds a bit closer about your shoulders.

My Robe is truth, also. As you wear it, you look at the world manifest from the heights we have attained, and you view, with true vision, the picture of man and his world. You see him in Truth also a part of Me, a part of the whole. You see and understand how he has brought to himself the burdens he carries and the troubles he bears, and you long to shield him with the ''Robe'' you wear.

Patience, forbearance, Love—all are qualities which you now wear as My garment. There is protection for you from outer winds as you use these qualities and as you know them for what they are, ''the qualities of Spirit within you.'' I would have you cast aside completely the dark, heavy garments with which you started the journey. They are unfit for these finer, lighter airs. The old robe of fear—cast it aside forever. You need never again to feel its weight upon you; likewise the Robe of distrust, selfishness, criticism; have done with this forever.

What a sense of freedom, of sureness and warmth

do you now have as, wearing the new Robe, you again take up the journey—going still higher with Me. My Robe shall never wear out; it constantly renews itself. If, when you first put it on, it looked to you plain and too simple to be of worth, yet as days pass and it is worn regally, it shall begin to glow with the hues of the rainbow and sparkle as if covered with gems.

Come, let us be on our way, knowing that together we wear the Robe of Love and Truth, My Robe of Righteousness.

SILENCE

MANY WORDS and much speaking do not denote consciousness. In the higher realms of consciousness where I am guiding you day by day, there is much silence. There is much power in silence, none in mere loud clamor. In former lessons we have spoken of the Great Silent Power of the Universe, and once again do I repeat, *"Silence is Power."*

As you go about your work on the physical plane, learn to put this precept into practice. Be silent when you sense a disagreement of others with your teachings. Be silent, that you confuse them not. Be silent when it would be but idle chatter for you to speak.

Learn to conserve energy for the time when the word spoken by Me through you shall bear fruit.

This lesson is not an easy one. It is so much easier to lend yourself to idle conversation which profiteth no one anything.

As you climb a mountain in the outer world, you find that as you go higher, you talk less and waste no strength in idle gestures, for you need all your energy to make the ascent. So it is with the "climbing" Soul into the higher altitudes of Spiritual consciousness. You find you will need times for quietness, for repose with Me, and you will often withdraw from clamor and confusion and give it not of your attention. You will keep your poise, quietly, gently, both within the Soul's depths and outwardly in your physical expression. You will waste no soul strength nor physical energy. At all times hold in reserve the qualities of power which I have given to you.

Be still in our union of Love, and I promise you, in time of need, that when it is necessary for you to use this strength, you will have an unlimited supply.

Remember this, My Beloved, for today and all days: much empty speaking only tends to add to body consciousness and decreases consciousness of Soul. Without Soul consciousness, you flounder about in all the ills and misfortunes, the mistakes and confusion of the merely physical being.

Go on about your tasks, but never fail to turn often to Me to renew your strength with the quietness of My Presence.

ACCEPT MY WORDS

MY BELOVED, this morning as I speak to you I ask you to accept these My words, which have been given to you, Soul. They are the outline for our journey into realms of a higher consciousness. This book is your map, and if carefully studied it shall serve you well.

It has marked for you both high points in consciousness and the pitfalls along the way. I have shown you beauty which shall greet your eyes as you attain the heights. The music of My spheres shall fill your ears, and the heavenly odors of My Presence shall cling to your garments when you have ascended to this peak of attainment.

Also, My child, I have deemed it necessary to show you the darkness of the pits into which you can fall, unless you are earnest and careful to keep steadfast the faith and fulfill the higher teachings. There are pits of negative thinking and speaking which will bring fear and discouragement in their wake. There are also pits of idle conversation and other faults of greater or less degree with the effects which will follow them. Avoid these pitfalls, My child, as you climb the trail. You need not stumble into them if you cling to My hand, keeping your eyes ever lifted toward the summit, to which you are making your journey.

I have also given you the password, *Love*. When you come to barriers across your way, use the word freely and forcefully and nothing shall hinder your progress. You will be shown flowers of attainment which will bloom for you as you do well the tasks of the day and as you live largely and freely as a child of the Father who holds all good in His hands for you.

So, Beloved, take for your use these My words that are so lovingly given to you. As you hold them to your heart and follow their gentle guidance, we shall grow very near, and you will know Me as the One Reality of your Soul. The way will not be a tedious one, but a joy-filled journey as it opens up before you.

My blessing is with you, and when you have the fullness of My protecting Love, you will have no fear. Keep your light burning, and others who struggle up the path shall see it shining, and it will make for them a journey of joy also.

Again, I bless you and say that as you go forth from this tryst each day, know that the Master journeys with you to the mountaintop of the Higher Consciousness.

EPILOGUE

THE MAN WHO CLIMBED TO GOD

T HE MAN was told that on the mountaintop he would find God, that there he would meet Him face to face. So the man arose early, before the light of day, and started on his journey. When the first rays of the sun came through the forest trees, it gave him joy, and he climbed steadily for many hours.

As he climbed, he became thirsty and sought a brook where he could quench his thirst, and while resting beside it, he fell asleep. As he slept, God came down from the mountaintop, and His form was that of a young man, strong of stature, with eyes of piercing beauty. God spoke. His voice rang out as a clear sweet bell. These are the words He spoke:

You started the journey of the Soul, away from the crowded cities with their glamor and deceit, away from the rush of life as it is lived by man in his ignorance. You came alone to the Mountain Trail as day dawned in your consciousness of what life really means. You entered on the way of the lonely ones, thinking if you kept to the path, up

*and over the crags of old beliefs and old desires,
that at last you would find Me, God. But I wait
not there in My high place of glory, while you
make the weary journey alone. I saw the desire.
burning in your Heart, as even now the sun burns
your flesh, and I hastened down to meet you, that
together we might make the journey back, from
Sense to Soul. The way, after all, will not be a
lonely one, for on every step of the way you shall
have Celestial Companionship. Awake! Rise up!
Let us be on Our way with joy.*

The man awakened and found he had slept through
the hours of the day and the soft evening dews were
upon his cheeks. The sky was jeweled with stars; there
was great stillness, and behold! He was even then
upon the mountaintop! He knew that God was there,
and within his heart was a great silence, and there,
within his own heart, dwelt God. He sang with joy,
for he had found a great secret: that where there is
stillness within, there can God be always found.

So he spent the night on the mountaintop in quiet
meditation, and with the day's dawning he went down
the trail to the busy city; but God went with him, and
the man walked and talked with God as they walked
the busy streets.

He was filled with Peace, for he had found that the
mountaintop was his own Soul's awakening at last to
the reality of its true being, and never again would he
have to search for God.